NAVAJO
CODE TALKERS

THIS EDITION

Editorial Management by Oriel Square
Produced for DK by WonderLab Group LLC
Jennifer Emmett, Erica Green, Kate Hale, *Founders*

Editor Maya Myers; **Photography Editor** Nicole DiMella; **Managing Editor** Rachel Houghton;
Designers Project Design Company; **Researcher** Michelle Harris;
Copy Editor Lori Merritt; **Indexer** Connie Binder; **Proofreader** Susan K. Hom;
Sensitivity Reader Dr. Naomi R. Caldwell; **Series Reading Specialist** Dr. Jennifer Albro; **Navajo Code Talker Historian** Zonnie M. Gorman;
Navajo Language Consultants Geneva Johnson, Roselyn Johnson

First American Edition, 2024
Published in the United States by DK Publishing, a division of Penguin Random House LLC
1745 Broadway, 20th Floor, New York, NY 10019

Copyright © 2024 Dorling Kindersley Limited
24 25 26 27 10 9 8 7 6 5 4 3 2 1
001–339769–Mar/2024

A catalog record for this book is available from the Library of Congress.
HC ISBN: 978-0-7440-9448-0
PB ISBN: 978-0-7440-9447-3

DK books are available at special discounts when purchased in bulk for sales promotions, premiums, fund-raising, or educational use. For details, contact:
DK Publishing Special Markets, 1745 Broadway, 20th Floor, New York, NY 10019
SpecialSales@dk.com

Printed and bound in China

The publisher would like to thank the following for their kind permission to reproduce their images: a=above; c=center; b=below; l=left; r=right; t=top; b/g=background

Alamy Stock Photo: Abaca Press 43br, Associated Press 50cb, 57br, Associated Press / Anonymous 46–47, Associated Press / Greg Sorber 46tl, Associated Press / Richard Drew 18tl, Hemis / Dozier Marc 16cla, Hemis / Frilet Patrick 7l, Hemis / Lemaire Stphane 54r, History and Art Collection 24bc, Dan Leeth 18–19, WorldPhotos 41tr, ZUMA Press, Inc. 52r; **Arizona State Library:** United States Marine Corps 28–29b, 48–49; **Barbara Billey:** 54bl; **Danielle Burbank:** 14cla, 56tl; **Courtesy of the Crow Canyon Archaeological Center:** Map by Neal Morris 19b; **Desiree Deschine:** 10t; **Dreamstime.com:** Blondsteve 17br, Brandon Bourdages 44–45t, Daniil Bukhta 27crb (Eggs), Chris Dorney 49cra, Ginosphotos / R. Gino Santa Maria / Shutterfree,Llc 24tl, Hakoar 50tl, Elena Istomina 31cra, Konstantin32 50–51b, Alain Lacroix 33tr, Luckyphotographer 30–31b, Nattaya Makerd 8r, Anastasia Maslova 25br, Mike7777777 31tr, Neutrino89 33cra, Sean Pavone 20–21b, Pleshko74 44cla, Pytyczech 7ca, Alexander Ryabintsev 42cla, Anna Shalygina 13cra, Nina Sitkevich 37cra, Tarasdubov 39crb, Wavemovies 39tr; **DVIDS:** Lance Cpl. Leslie Alcaraz 56–57t, Cpl. Kathryn Bynum 29tr, Coast Guard Photo / Chief Petty Officer Bob Laura 1, Cpl. Jason Jimenez 30tl, Done Jones 23tr, Hun Chustine Minoda 16–17tc; **Jay Galvin:** 20t; **Getty Images:** AFP / Mike Theiler 55tl, Archive Photos / Interim Archives 38tl, 41b, Bettmann 28tl, Corbis Historical / Steven Clevenger 58tl, Denver Post / Lyn Alweis 55tr, Gamma-Rapho / Sylvain Grandadam 52tl, Hearst Newspapers / Houston Chronicle 4–5, Chip Somodevilla 8tl, Universal Images Group / Windmill Books 12tl; **Getty Images / iStock:** Coolvectormaker 27crb, DigitalVision Vectors / designer29 13cra (Flag), E+ / grandriver 14br, E+ / RichVintage 25tr, Ericbvd 6 (Background), 61 (Background), fcknimages 21tr, Godruma 37crb (tortoise), Mochipet 13cra (notebook), 25br (notebook), 27crb (notebook), 31br (notebook), 37r (x2), 39r (X2), 42tl, 44cla (notebook), TopVectors 44cla (Explosive), Wissanu99 31br, 37cra (ship), 37crb, 39cra, 42cla (air force), zelimirz 39br; **Gorman Family Collection:** 53tr; **Image Courtesy of International Military Antiques, Inc. IMA-USA.com:** 40b; **LaVerne Johnson:** 6b, 60bc, 61b; **Library of Congress, Washington, D.C.:** Haines Photo Co. , Copyright Claimant. U.S. Indian School, Carlisle, Penna. Pennsylvania United States Carlisle, ca. 1909. Photograph. https: // www.loc.gov / item / 2007661485 / . 24–25t, Carol M Highsmith 56bl, Frances Benjamin Johnston 22–23b, Ready--Join U.S. Marines / Sundblom. , 1942. [Camden, N.J.: Alpha Litho. Co] Photograph. https: / www.loc.gov / item / 93500072 / . 9tr; **National Museum of the American Indian, Smithsonian Institution:** 55br; **Northern Arizona University:** 11tr; **Shutterstock.com:** Jon Freeman 45tr, Sergey Kamshylin 3, Lora liu 36cr, 58r; **U.S. Air Force:** 27tr; **U.S. Government Accountability Office:** 7tc; **United States Marine Corps:** 12–13b, 32–33t, 39cl; **The US National Archives and Records Administration:** 9bl, 11b, 15b, 26–27b, 32tl, 35, 37bl, 38br, 42br, 42–43tc, 45tl, 47tr, 59b

Cover images: *Front:* **Getty Images:** Archive Photos / Interim Archives (Background); **The US National Archives and Records Administration:** Navajo Indian Code Talkers Henry Bake and George Kirk; 12 / 1943; Photographs of Navajo Indian "Code-Talkers" in the U.S. Marine Corps, 1943 - 1948; Records of the U.S. Marine Corps, Record Group 127; National Archives at College Park, College Park, MD. b; *Back:* **Alamy Stock Photo:** Irwin Seidman cra; **Shutterstock.com:** Militarist clb

All other images © Dorling Kindersley
For more information see: www.dkimages.com

www.dk.com

Publisher's note: Different words can be used for groups of people who are indigenous to a place. This series uses terms preferred by members of the group being discussed.

Level
4

NAVAJO
CODE TALKERS

Danielle C. Burbank

CONTENTS

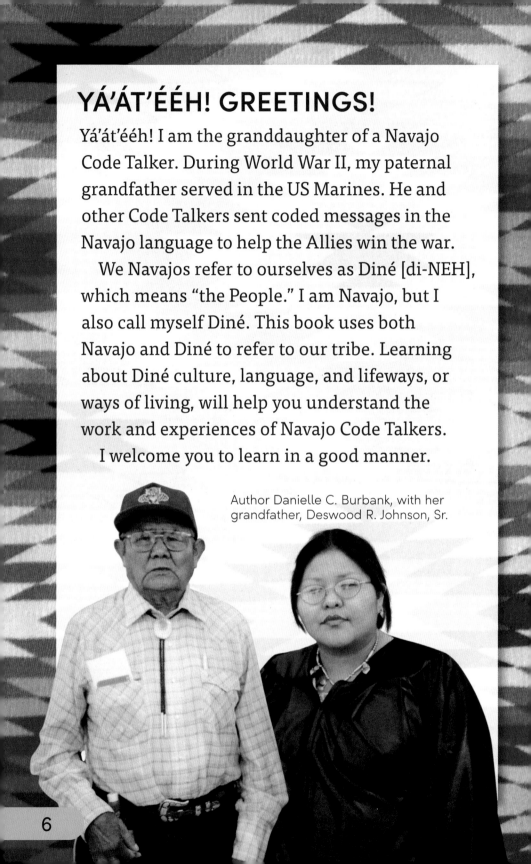

YÁ'ÁT'ÉÉH! GREETINGS!

Yá'át'ééh! I am the granddaughter of a Navajo Code Talker. During World War II, my paternal grandfather served in the US Marines. He and other Code Talkers sent coded messages in the Navajo language to help the Allies win the war.

We Navajos refer to ourselves as Diné [di-NEH], which means "the People." I am Navajo, but I also call myself Diné. This book uses both Navajo and Diné to refer to our tribe. Learning about Diné culture, language, and lifeways, or ways of living, will help you understand the work and experiences of Navajo Code Talkers.

I welcome you to learn in a good manner.

Author Danielle C. Burbank, with her grandfather, Deswood R. Johnson, Sr.

Navajo Nation

Utah   Colorado

Arizona

New Mexico

Navajo Nation

The Navajo Nation is one of the largest tribal nations in the United States. The Diné homelands are located in what is now Arizona, New Mexico, and Utah. Approximately 173,000 people live on the Navajo Nation, and there are about 400,000 Diné tribal members.

Navajo Greetings

In the Navajo [NA-vuh-ho] language, yá'át'ééh [yah-ah-t-AY] is a formal greeting. The word yá'át'ééh translates to "it is good." This greeting sets the stage for people to welcome one another in a good manner.

NAVAJO CODE TALKERS

Have you ever written a coded message, one that only someone else who knew your secret code would understand? Can you use the chart below to figure out the coded words?

Check your answers on p. 64.

Other Native Language Codes
During World War I, the Comanche and Choctaw languages were used by the US Army to deliver messages. About 25 other Native nations used their Native languages during both World Wars. The Navajo were the first to create a special code using their language for the Marine Corps.

A	B	C	D	E	F	G	H	I	J	K	L	M
N	O	P	Q	R	S	T	U	V	W	X	Y	Z

1.

_____ ?

2.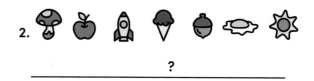

_____ ?

3.

_____ ?

Secret codes were very important during World War II.

Navajo Code Talkers were specially trained Marines who used their language to help keep information secret during World War II. Twenty-nine young Navajo men helped to create an unbreakable code in their Diné language. By the end of the war, about 420 Navajo Code Talkers were sending secret messages.

World War II
World War II was fought between 1939 and 1945, between two groups of countries known as the Allies and the Axis powers. The United States entered the war in 1941, the day after the bombing of Pearl Harbor in Hawaii.

Navajo Code Talkers PFC Edmund J. Henry, Sr., PFC Wilsie H. Bitsie, and PFC Eugene R. Crawford, New Georgia, Solomon Islands, 1943

Sign at Dream Diné School in Shiprock, New Mexico, pointing to the sacred mountains

Navajo Alphabet

Over the years, English speakers made many attempts to write Navajo words using an English alphabet. But the Navajo language has sounds that are unlike sounds in the English language. New characters had to be developed to represent these sounds.

Why was the Navajo language so good for making a secret code? At the time of World War II, the Navajo population was around 50,000 people. Few non-Navajo spoke or understood the Navajo language. Many Navajos considered English a foreign language.

Some English speakers attempted to write down the Navajo language, but there was not a common version of written Navajo.

A man named Philip Johnston grew up on the Navajo reservation as a child of missionaries. He was not Navajo, but he spoke some of the Navajo language. Johnston understood how remote and isolated reservation life was.

Johnston knew about other Native Americans using their language during World War I. He believed the Navajo language could be used to help deliver important messages that no one else could understand. He convinced the US Marines that the Navajo language could assist with the war.

Philip Johnston (right) with a Navajo friend, 1941

(288)
1535
15/11-jwa

HEADQUARTERS,
AMPHIBIOUS FORCE, PACIFIC FLEET,
CAMP ELLIOTT, SAN DIEGO, CALIFORNIA

March 6, 1942

From: The Commanding General.
To: The Commandant, U. S. Marine Corps.

Subject: Enlistment of Navaho Indians.

Enclosures: (A) Brochure by Mr. Philip Johnston, with maps.
               (B) Messages used in demonstration.

1.   Mr. Philip Johnston of Los Angeles recently offered his services to this force to demonstrate the use of Indians for the transmission of messages by telephone and voice-radio. His offer was accepted and the demonstration was held for the Commanding General and his staff.

2.   The demonstration was interesting ar̲ ̲ ̲ ̲ ̲ ̲ ̲were transmitted and received almos̲. ̲ ̲ ̲ ̲ ̲ ̲ ̲ ̲messages were written by a ̲ ̲ ̲ ̲ ̲ ̲would trans̲

Cryptography
Coded messages can help keep information private during combat. Things like locations, movement of troops, and orders need to be shared in a way that can only be understood by those fighting together on one side of a war. World War II happened decades before the internet or cell phones were invented. Back then, it was a lot harder to send messages than it is today.

The Navajo code was specifically designed and created by the First 29 Navajo Code Talkers. The First 29 did not have any formal training in making codes, yet they devised a Navajo code dictionary and used it to help win the war.

The Navajo Code Talkers were bilingual. They could speak and understand both Navajo and English. They learned English in

382nd PLATOON

school. Navajo was their first language, which they learned with their families.

Diné language, culture, and tradition gave the Code Talkers unique skills to help them succeed at the challenging task they were given. What did they learn from their families, communities, and schools that helped them carry out this important secret mission?

NAVAJO
**nihimá
[NE-HE-MAH]**

ENGLISH
our mother

CODE FOR
United States

You can learn some words from the Navajo Code Talker Dictionary! Here, the modern Navajo spelling is followed by the phonetic spelling used in the Navajo Code Talker Dictionary, then the English translation of that word, and the thing the word was code for.

The First 29 with officers; the first all-Navajo platoon in the history of the US Marine Corps

C. SAN DIEGO
2

The author's daughter and her paternal great-grandmother

Four Clans
Each Navajo has four clans: the families of their mother, father, maternal grandfather, and paternal grandfather. Navajo is a matrilineal society, so a person's mother's clan is their main clan. Clanship strengthens family ties and k'é.

DINÉ LIFEWAYS

Navajo Code Talkers came to the Marines with a lifetime of practicing Diné lifeways. Lifeways are ways of using traditional knowledge to understand the world. For Diné, traditional knowledge includes a deep understanding of family, land, and life.

An important teaching for Diné is k'é [keh], or kinship. The general rule of k'é is to establish respect and compassion for one another. Kinship is how Diné create relationships through their clans, or families. Kinship helped the Navajo Code Talkers bond with one another and with their fellow Marines.

Navajo kinship is based in oral tradition. For generations, Diné have repeated aloud their stories, songs, and prayers. Diné people learn from their family members through repetition and memorization. These skills proved to be very important for the Navajo Code Talkers, who would have to memorize their code.

Code Talker Leslie Hemstreet playing a drum in Okinawa, 1945

Oral Tradition
A culture that practices oral tradition passes stories and lessons from generation to generation by telling them aloud rather than writing them down. Oral tradition includes songs, prayers, and stories.

Code Talker Thomas Begay at the Navajo Nation Fair parade, 2014

Tribal Identity
The idea of balance is especially important to people who maintain their identity as Diné and as citizens of the United States. Native Americans were not recognized as US citizens until 1924, but they have always maintained their tribal identity, as well as their love and respect for their homelands.

The Navajo cultural belief of maintaining balance is called hózhǫ́ [HO-zhoh]. Hózhǫ́ means harmony, beauty, and balance. There are many prayers and songs based on this concept in Navajo beliefs. The Code Talkers' knowledge of hózhǫ́ helped them maintain balance in an ever-changing world.

Tribal Affiliation
The terms Native American, American Indian, and Indigenous can all be used to express racial identity. But rather than using these broad terms to label an individual person, if possible, it is best to acknowledge their specific tribe or tribes. Some people have more than one tribal affiliation.

One way the Code Talkers maintained a connection to the land during the war was with corn pollen. They carried corn pollen in small leather bags. They used it when they prayed for protection. Many Navajo Code Talkers mentioned keeping their corn pollen near them during war time.

The Navajo Code Talkers were from Diné Bikéyah [di-NEH bi-KAY-yuh], their Diné homelands. The homelands lie between four sacred mountains. Diné believe this is where creation, known as the emergence, happened. Many Diné stories, songs, and prayers are tied to the four sacred mountains and the land. Diné homelands hold a spiritual connection and kinship between people, the land, animals, plants, and other spiritual beings.

Mount Hesperus, Colorado

The Navajo Code Talkers continued to practice these beliefs even beyond the boundaries of their Diné homelands. During the war, they wanted to protect all land and humanity to maintain hózhǫ́.

UTAH

COLORADO

Blanca Peak
(Sisnaajiní)

Hesperus Peak
(Dibé Ntsaa)

Mesa Verde Region

ARIZONA

San Francisco Peaks
(Dook'o'oslííd)

Flagstaff

NEW
MEXICO

Mt. Taylor
(Tsoodził)

Albuquerque

Long Walk Home mural in Gallup, New Mexico, by Richard Kee Yazzie

Tribal Nations
The Navajo Nation is one of 574 federally recognized American Indian and Alaska Native tribes throughout the United States. Each tribal nation has its own government, land, language, flag, and more.

As US Marines, the Navajo Code Talkers served to protect and defend the US. But these Diné men came to their service with complicated feelings about a US government that had taken their people from their homelands and tried to erase their culture.

In 1864, the US government forced more than 8,500 Diné elders, men, women, and children to march as far as 450 miles from their homelands to a fort where they were imprisoned for four years. Many Navajo people died during this march, called the Navajo Long Walk.

In 1868, the Diné were allowed to return to their homelands on a reservation within the four sacred mountains. However, the reservation was significantly smaller than their original homelands.

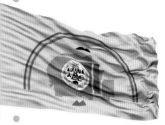

Reservations
Many tribal nations exist today on lands called a reservation. Many tribes were forced by the US government from their original homelands onto reservations. More than 300 reservations in 35 states cover as much as 100 million acres of land.

Shiprock, New Mexico

Fort Sumner
The Diné called Fort Sumner, New Mexico, where they were held for four years, Hwéeldi [WHAYL-di]—the place of grief and suffering.

21

SCHOOLS ON THE RESERVATION

Once the Diné were allowed to return to their homelands, the US government still dictated a lot about what they did, including how, when, and where their children went to school. Children on the Navajo reservation had to attend government and religious boarding schools.

Male Native American students in physical education class, Carlisle Indian School

The boarding schools were highly influenced by the military. Some of the schools were even located in old forts or military sites on reservations. Life at boarding schools was shaped by discipline and rule-following. For the young men who became Code Talkers, this was fitting preparation for a military lifestyle.

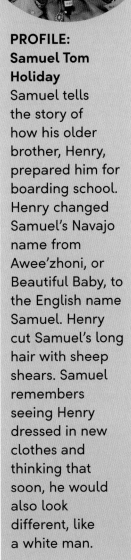

PROFILE: Samuel Tom Holiday
Samuel tells the story of how his older brother, Henry, prepared him for boarding school. Henry changed Samuel's Navajo name from Awee'zhoni, or Beautiful Baby, to the English name Samuel. Henry cut Samuel's long hair with sheep shears. Samuel remembers seeing Henry dressed in new clothes and thinking that soon, he would also look different, like a white man.

Erasing Native Culture

Native American boarding schools were not safe places where children could be themselves. The people who ran the schools believed their culture was better than Native culture and that Native culture should be erased. They thought they were helping children, but they were hurting them.

The intent of Native American boarding schools was to assimilate Native children into American culture and strip away their Native identity. Often, their own names were replaced with English names. The children were forced to cut their hair and wear unfamiliar clothing. They were taken from their families and kept away from their communities and traditions.

Band and battalion at Carlisle Indian School

Carlisle Indian School, Carlisle, Pennsylvania

In these schools, the children were forced to speak only English. They could be beaten for using their Native languages. And yet, the same government that tried to erase their language would recruit young men from these very schools and ask them to use their Native language to help the government win a war.

Bringing Language Back Today, the Navajo language is taught in most schools on the Navajo Nation. Language immersion schools focus on Navajo language, and other schools encourage Navajo cultural teachings.

NAVAJO
**gáagii
[GA-GIH]**

ENGLISH
crow

CODE FOR
**patrol
plane**

Enigma
While the Code Talkers fought in the Pacific, World War II was also being fought in Europe. The Germans had an encryption machine called Enigma that could generate a coded alphabet to send a message.

ENTERING WORLD WAR II

The United States entered World War II on December 8, 1941. The day before, the US naval base at Pearl Harbor in Hawaii had been bombed by the Japanese.

During the war, sending messages in secret was important. At the time, messages were sent through radio or by telephone. The Japanese were skilled at breaking codes and other forms of secret communication. The Allies needed an unbreakable code.

Over the course of the war, machines were developed specifically to send encrypted, or coded, messages. But machines were sometimes broken or tampered with. A code developed and used by a select few people, however, proved to be efficient and unbreakable.

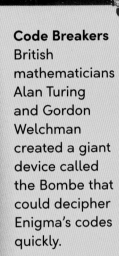

Code Breakers British mathematicians Alan Turing and Gordon Welchman created a giant device called the Bombe that could decipher Enigma's codes quickly.

Pearl Harbor,
December 7, 1941

NAVAJO
ayęęzhii [A-YE-SHI]

ENGLISH
eggs

CODE FOR
bomb

Drafted or Enlisted?

During the war, many individuals chose to enlist to help in the conflict. However, many more were drafted, which meant that their service was mandatory. Some of the Navajo Code Talkers were drafted, while some chose to enlist.

When the US entered the war, they needed more soldiers. And once the Marines decided to try using a Navajo code, they needed Navajos to serve as Code Talkers. The Marines recruited Navajo students from the boarding schools on or near the reservation. These students were all able to read and write in English, and they still spoke and understood Navajo.

The Marines wanted men between 17 and 32 years old. A lot of young men lied about their ages, but since many Navajos were born at home without birth certificates, their ages were hard to prove. The Marines needed their help, so they weren't too strict about this rule.

Navajo men being inducted into the US Marine Corps at Fort Wingate, New Mexico, 1942

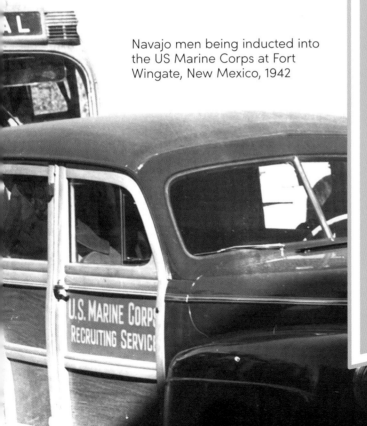

PROFILE:
Chester Nez
Chester was one of the First 29 recruits in 1942. When he was 18, the school principal at Tuba City Boarding School told the students about Pearl Harbor and the war. Chester recalls Marine recruiters looking for young Navajo men for a special project. Chester and Roy Begay, his roommate, made the decision to join the Marines.

Navajo Code Talkers have often been questioned about why they wanted to fight in a war to help the US government—the same government that removed the Diné from their homelands and forced them to attend boarding schools.

PROFILE:
Thomas H. Begay
Thomas believes he was protected during the war because of his traditional Diné upbringing. His family held ceremonies for his protection. Thomas knows these ceremonies protected his overall well-being. When Thomas was sent to replace a Code Talker who had been killed in action, he saw his service as an act of restoring balance.

War creates an imbalance for individuals and their connection to their homelands. War goes against hózhǫ́, the traditional Diné teaching of balance. Some Navajo Code Talkers enlisted in order to restore balance, protect their homelands, and help end the war.

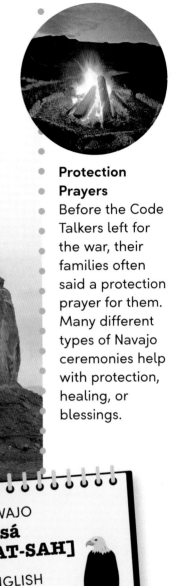

Protection Prayers
Before the Code Talkers left for the war, their families often said a protection prayer for them. Many different types of Navajo ceremonies help with protection, healing, or blessings.

Hunts Mesa, Arizona

NAVAJO
atsá
[AT-SAH]

ENGLISH
eagle

CODE FOR
transport plane

Navajo Code Talkers training at Camp Pendleton, California, 1942

First 29 Recruits
The First 29 were sworn into the Marine Corps on May 4, 1942, at Fort Wingate, New Mexico. They graduated from boot camp in June, then worked on developing the Navajo code. By August 1942, they were sent into combat.

The First 29 recruits left the Navajo Nation and traveled by bus to California. There, they had to endure seven weeks of basic training, also known as "boot camp." They faced many rigorous and difficult challenges, both physical and mental. The harsh conditions of their upbringing on the reservation and in the boarding schools helped them persevere.

Then, the Navajo Marines were taken to Camp Elliott in California

for a top secret mission—even *they* still didn't know exactly what they would be doing. They were told they would learn to use radio and telephone equipment. They assumed they would learn military communications, like Morse code.

And they did learn Morse code, as well as semaphore, a system of communicating using flags. They learned to operate field telephones and heavy portable radios. But they were not there only to learn. Their mission was about to be revealed to them.

Morse Code
In the 1830s, American inventor Samuel Morse created a form of coded communication that uses dots, dashes, and spaces for letters of the alphabet to transmit a message.

Why Navajo?
Navajo was chosen because of its complex sounds and tones. A lot of the sounds in Navajo language come from the nose or throat. The meaning of a word can easily change if it's pronounced incorrectly.

CRAFTING A DICTIONARY

At last, the 29 freshly trained Marines were told their true mission: they were to use their Diné bizaad [din-EH bi-ZAHD], their Navajo language, to create a secret code.

The men were shocked. For many years in boarding school, they had been prohibited from speaking their language. Now, they were being told to use that language to create a code that could help win the war.

Because these Diné men came from a culture that relied on oral tradition, their language and memorization skills were strong.

Their first task was to create an alphabet.

Cousins PFC Preston Toledo (left) and PFC Frank Toledo relaying orders over a field radio in the South Pacific using the Navajo code

The Code Talkers used the English alphabet to spell out Navajo words. They spelled the words phonetically, or the way they sounded. Because of this, the way Navajo words look in the Code Talker Dictionary is different from the way those words look in today's Navajo language.

The First 29 Code Talkers started by creating a code for the English alphabet. Each letter of the alphabet was associated with one or more words in Navajo, but the word in Navajo didn't always start with the same letter as the English word. So, for example, if they wanted to send the word READ, the code might be:

GAH AH-JAH WOL-LA-CHEE BE

GAH = R = rabbit

AH-JAH = E = ear

WOL-LA-CHEE = A = ant

BE = D = deer

Note that the Navajo words have different first letters than the English translation words do. This gave the Navajo code a double layer of encryption. So, each letter could be represented by several different words.

The Navajo Code Talker Dictionary also used word association, or whole words that stood for other things. For example, the Navajo word for WHALE, LO-TSO, meant BATTLESHIP. There were words to represent military phrases, officers' names, countries, airplanes, ships, and more. The Code Talkers used words they knew from the reservation, like the names for animals and land formations. Airplanes were named after birds. Different types of ships were named after fish or sea life.

NAVAJO
łóó'tsoh [LO-TSO]

ENGLISH
whale

CODE FOR
battleship

NAVAJO
ch'ééh digháhii [CHAY-DA-GAHI]

ENGLISH
tortoise

CODE FOR
tank

REVISED AS OF 15 JUNE, 1945.

UNCLASSIFIED NAVAJO DICTIONARY

ALPHABET

A.	(WOL-LA-CHEE)	ANT	K.	(KLIZZIE-YAZZIE)	KID
A.	(BE-LA-SANA)	APPLE	L.	(DIBEH-YAZZIE)	LAMB
A.	(TSE-NILL)	AXE	L.	(AH-JAD)	LEG
B.	(NA-HASH-CHID)	BADGER	L.	(NASH-DOIE-TSO)	LION
B.	(SHUSH)	BEAR	M.	(TSIN-TLITI)	MATCH
B.	(TOISH-JEH)	BARREL	M.	(BE-TAS-TNI)	MIRROR
C.	(MOASI)	CAT	M.	(NA-AS-TSO-SI)	MOUSE
C.	(TLA-GIN)	COAL	N.	(TSAH)	NEEDLE
C.	(BA-GOSHI)	COW	N.	(A-CHIN)	NOSE
D.	(BE)	DEER	O.	(A-KHA)	OIL
D.	(CHINDI)	DEVIL	O.	(TLO-CHIN)	ONION
D.	(LHA-CHA-EH)	DOG	O.	(NE-AHS-JAH)	OWL
E.	(AH-JAH)	EAR	P.	(CLA-GI-AIH)	PANT
E.	(DZEH)	ELK	P.	(BI-SO-DIH)	PIG
E.	(AH-NAH)	EYE	P.	(NE-ZHONI)	PRETTY
F.	(CHUO)	FIR	Q.	(CA-YEILTH)	QUIVER
F.	(TSA-E-DONIN-EE)	FLY	R.	(GAH)	RABBIT
F.	(MA-E)	FOX	R.	(DAH-NES-TSA)	RAM
G.	(AH-TAD)	GIRL	R.	(AH-LOSZ)	RICE
G.	(KLIZZIE)	GOAT	S.	(DIBEH)	SHEEP
G.	(JEHA)	GUM	S.	(KLESH)	SNAKE
H.	(TSE-GAH)	HAIR	T.	(D-AH)	TEA
H.	(CHA)	HAT	T.	(A-WOH)	TOOTH
H.	(LIN)	HORSE	T.	(THAN-ZIE)	TURKEY
I.	(TKIN)	ICE	U.	(SHI-DA)	UNCLE
I.	(YEH-HES)	ITCH	U.	(NO-DA-IH)	UTE
I.	(A-CHI)	INTESTINE	V.	(A-KEH-DI-GLINI)	VICTOR
J.	(TKELE-CHO-GI)	JACKASS	W.	(CLOE-IH)	WEASEL
J.	(AH-YA-TSINNE)	JAW	X.	(AL-NA-AS-DZOH)	CROSS
J.	(YIL-DOI)	JERK	Y.	(TSAH-AS-ZIH)	YUCCA
K.	(JAD-HO-LONI)	KETTLE	Z.	(BESH-DO-TLIZ)	ZINC
K.	(BA-AH-NE-DI-TININ)	KEY			

A.	ABLE	J.	JIG	S.	SUGAR
B.	BAKER	K.	KING	T.	TARE
C.	CHARLIE	L.	LOVE	U.	UNCLE
D.	DOG	M.	MIKE	V.	VICTOR
E.	EASY	N.	NAN	W.	WILLIAM
F.	FOX	O.	OBOE	X.	X-RAY
G.	GEORGE	P.	PETER	Y.	YOKE
H.	HOW	Q.	QUEEN	Z.	ZEBRA
I.	ITEM	R.	ROGER		

Secret Code
Even Navajo-speaking soldiers who were not trained as Code Talkers could not figure out the code. They could understand the words but not why the words were put together in the order they were. It sounded like nonsense. The code only made sense to the Code Talkers.

At first, the Navajo Code Talker Dictionary had about 200 words. As the war progressed, the conflict expanded to new locations. New technologies and weapons came into use. More code words were needed. In the end, the dictionary had nearly 700 entries.

The Code Talkers could not risk carrying a printed copy of their dictionary. If they were taken captive and the enemy learned the code, the code would become useless. So, the Code Talkers had to commit the entire thing to memory. The oral traditions of their Diné culture helped them to memorize it.

Rear: Pvt Jack C. Morgan, Pvt George H. Kirk, Sr.; Pvt Tom H. Jones; Cpl Henry Bahe, Jr. Front: Pvt Earl Johnny, Pvt Kee Etsicitty, Pvt John V. Goodluck, PFC David Jordan. Bouganville Island, December 1943

After the First 29 Navajo Code Talkers crafted the dictionary, they demonstrated how it should be used. The Marines found the Code Talkers' techniques effective and efficient. They proceeded to recruit, draft, and train around 400 more Navajo men to become Code Talkers. Then, the Code Talkers were sent into combat.

NAVAJO
bééshłóó'
[BESH-LO]

ENGLISH
iron fish

CODE FOR
submarine

The second all-Navajo Marine platoon

NAVAJO
táchii'nii
[TACHEENE]

ENGLISH
red soil

CODE FOR
battalion

CODE TALKERS IN COMBAT

After their training, 27 of the First 29 were deployed or sent to areas in the Pacific where the war was being fought. The other two Code Talkers stayed in the US to help recruit and train more Code Talkers.

From 1942 to 1945, Navajo Code Talkers served throughout the Marine Corps. They traveled by ship for several weeks, then landed on the shores of different battlefields throughout the Pacific Theater. They fought in every major battle during this period.

Radio Equipment
The Code Talkers used 50-pound radios to transmit their messages. Each radio had four different parts: a transmitter, a receiver, a battery, and wiring. Today, of course, the same job could be done with a cell phone so small it can fit in a pocket.

The Code Talkers worked in pairs, sending messages on heavy portable radios. One of them would receive a message written in English from an officer. He would read the message, then encrypt it, or turn it into Navajo code, in his head. Then, he would say the message through the radio in Navajo code to a Code Talker in another location. The other Code Talker would hear the Navajo message, decrypt it in his head, then write down the message in English. Navajo Code Talkers were much faster and more efficient than machines that could do the same job.

Pacific Theater
In wartime, a theater is a large area where the war is being fought. It includes sky, land, sea, and everything in between.

Marines in the Palau Islands, 1944

NAVAJO
dahiitįhii
[DA-HE-TIH-HI]

ENGLISH
hummingbird

CODE FOR
fighter plane

Corporal Oscar Ilthma and PFC Jack Nez, and PFC Carl Gorman, Saipan, 1944

When they were deployed in the Pacific Theater, Navajo Code Talkers were sometimes confused with Japanese soldiers because of similar physical or facial features. There are stories of Japanese soldiers stealing clothes from American soldiers to disguise themselves as Americans.

Code Talker Jimmy Benally in Okinawa, Japan, 1945

Other American troops were sometimes confused by the Navajo language, too. Some thought the Code Talkers were speaking Japanese.

To protect the Navajo Code Talkers, some were paired with non-Navajo bodyguards, or buddies. The buddies made sure other Americans knew that the Code Talkers were US Marines and not Japanese fighters.

NAVAJO
nímasii
[NI-MA-SI]

ENGLISH
potatoes

CODE FOR
grenade

One of the famous battles the Code Talkers were involved in was the Battle of Iwo Jima, which lasted for more than a month. During the first 48 hours of this battle, it is said they delivered 800 messages using the Navajo code without making any mistakes. They couldn't afford mistakes. A mistake could mean injury or death for many people.

United States Marine Corps War Memorial, Arlington, Virginia; inset: US Marines raising the US flag on Iwo Jima, 1945

The Code Talkers helped secure landing positions, confirmed troop locations, and reported injuries and deaths. Three Navajo Code Talkers were killed while helping US forces win this particular battle.

RETURNING HOME

The war ended in 1945. With the assistance of Navajo Code Talkers, the Allies had won. The Code Talkers were discharged, or released from their service, and sent home. But some of the Code Talkers chose to stay in the Marines. Some joined other branches of the military.

Being home on the reservation was difficult. The war had been hard on the economy in all of the US, but particularly on the reservation. The reservation lacked resources and infrastructure for

water, electricity, and other things that most of America had easy access to during that time. There were few opportunities for employment.

Many of the former Code Talkers moved away from the Navajo Nation. Some moved to bigger cities to find work. Many of the men returned to complete high school. Others enrolled in college or vocational school.

No matter what they did after the war, each of the Code Talkers carried a secret.

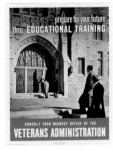

G.I. Bill
After World War II, the US government passed a law to provide benefits to military veterans. One of these benefits was financial assistance to pursue education. Many Code Talkers used this to further their education.

Hogan and stone house, Navajo reservation, Arizona, 1960

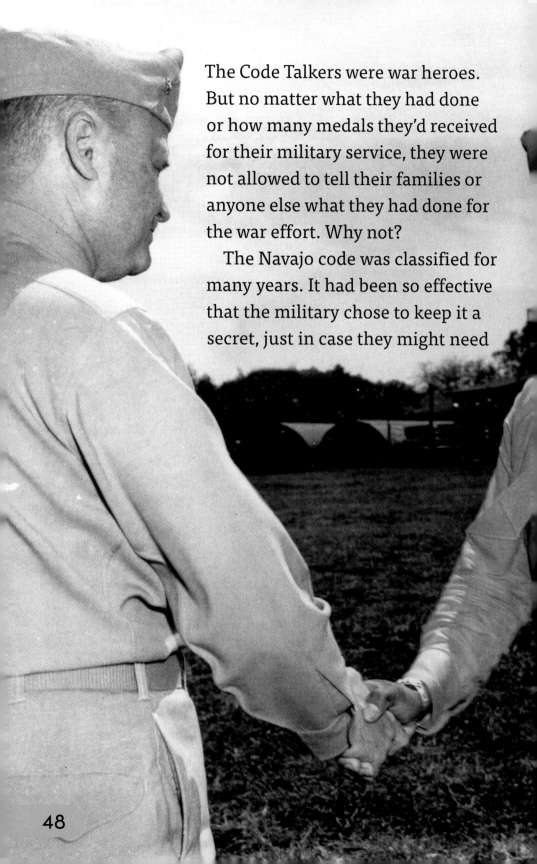

The Code Talkers were war heroes. But no matter what they had done or how many medals they'd received for their military service, they were not allowed to tell their families or anyone else what they had done for the war effort. Why not?

The Navajo code was classified for many years. It had been so effective that the military chose to keep it a secret, just in case they might need

to use it again in a future conflict. When the code was finally declassified in 1968, the Code Talkers had gone more than two decades without sharing their war experiences with their families and communities.

DECLASSIFIED

Declassified
Information that is kept secret is called classified. Only a few people are allowed to know about it. When information is declassified, it is is available for anyone to access.

Code Talker William Yazzie receiving a medal, 1947

Navajo Ceremonies
Many Navajo ceremonies are still practiced today. There are ceremonies for protection or blessings. A ceremony can last a few hours, but some last for up to nine nights. Navajo ceremonies are measured by nights, not days, because ceremonies are completed at dawn.

The secret the Code Talkers were forced to carry took a heavy toll on them. The death and destruction they had seen in the war caused an imbalance in their lives. Since they could not share their experiences freely, it was difficult to talk with family and friends about their time in the war.

US Army veteran Henry Whitehair, left, returning to his family's hogan on the Navajo Nation after serving in the Pacific Theater, 1945

Diné cultural upbringing helped many Code Talkers heal. Healing ceremonies cleansed their minds, warded off negativity, and restored balance. The ceremonies helped with things like nightmares, anxiety, and depression. Ceremonies gave them ways to cope with the traumas they had experienced.

Code Talker John V. Goodluck, 2006

Uniform
The yellow shirt of the Navajo Code Talkers Association uniform represents corn pollen, which is used ceremonially for blessings. The shirt is worn with khaki pants that represent the Marine Corps and the earth, and Navajo moccasins. Association members also adorn themselves with Navajo jewelry and a red hat, indicating their military service as Marines.

CELEBRATING HEROES

After the code was declassified in 1968, the Navajo Code Talkers began to tell their stories. Slowly, they gained recognition for their heroism.

Dr. Samuel Billison

In 1971, the surviving Code Talkers formed the Navajo Code Talkers Association. The association hoped to educate younger generations about their service as Code Talkers. Members of the association traveled around the country to show others how they used the code in combat. They participated in parades, school assemblies, and celebrations to educate others and share their wisdom.

It was an honor to hear these heroes speak the Diné language and stress the importance of continuing to speak Diné bizaad. They encouraged the revitalization of the Navajo language. They wanted younger Navajo kids to learn more about it in school. Even for fluent Navajo speakers, reading and writing the language would be something new, since Navajo had always been an oral language and not written. Today, many schools, from preschool through college, teach Navajo.

PROFILE:
Dr. Carl Gorman
Carl was one of the First 29. He attended the Otis Art Institute in Los Angeles on the G.I. Bill. He studied fine arts and then became a professor at the University of California–Davis, where he helped create the Native American Studies Department. He also designed the logo for the Navajo Code Talkers Association.

Wilfred was part of the second all-Navajo platoon of Code Talkers. After the war, he completed his education and became a teacher, school counselor, and high school principal. Wilfred helped ensure that the Navajo Code Talkers received their congressional medals and helped create the medal's inscription.

In 1982, August 14 was designated as National Navajo Code Talkers Day. August 14 is the date Japan surrendered during World War II. Each year, the Navajo Nation celebrates August 14 as a tribal holiday.

Code Talkers in the parade at the Navajo Nation Fair, Window Rock, Arizona, September 2014

President George W. Bush presenting Code Talker John Brown, Jr., with a medal, 2000

Congressional Medal
One side of the medal shows two Code Talkers. The other side displays the Navajo Code Talkers Association logo. The inscription reads, "Diné Bizaad Yee Atah Naayéé' Yik'eh Deesdl íí," which means "The Navajo Language Was Used to Defeat the Enemy."

In 2000, Congress passed the Honoring the Code Talkers Act. The First 29 were awarded Congressional Gold Medals. Five of them were still alive, and four traveled to Washington, DC, to receive their medals in person. Over 300 other Code Talkers received Congressional Silver Medals in Window Rock, Arizona, the capital of the Navajo Nation.

On Display
Statues in Gallup, New Mexico, and Phoenix, Arizona honor the Code Talkers. They are even honored with a creative display at a fast-food restaurant in Kayenta, Arizona!

Mural in Tonalea, Arizona

Navajo Code Talkers are also honored with memorial statues. At the Navajo Tribal Park & Veterans Memorial in Window Rock, Arizona, a large bronze statue includes a descriptive plaque. Its sculptor, Oreland Joe, of the Navajo and Ute tribes, was a former student of Navajo Code Talker Dr. Wilfred E. Billey.

Navajo Nation Marines at the Navajo Code Talker memorial, Window Rock, Arizona, 2022

Mixed Media
You can learn a lot about different Code Talker stories in books, movies, documentaries, websites, and more. The Veterans History Project, part of the Library of Congress's American Folklife Center, includes personal accounts by 21 Navajo Code Talkers.

Many books have been written about Navajo Code Talkers. In some of them, the Code Talkers themselves tell about their unique experiences in their own words.

Code Talker Bill Toledo signing books, 2022

The innovation, determination, and perseverance of the Navajo Code Talkers helped the Allies win World War II. But the memory and legacy of the Navajo Code Talkers is more than just their war efforts.

Code Talker Joe Vandever welcomes a veteran home, 2006

THE FIRST 29 NAVAJO CODE TALKERS

Charlie Begay

Roy L. Begay

Samuel Begay

John Ashi Benally

Wilsie H. Bitsie

Cosey Stanley Brown

John Brown, Jr.

John Chee

Benjamin Cleveland

Eugene Roanhorse Crawford

David Curley

Lowell Smith Damon

George H. Dennison

James Dixon

Carl Nelson Gorman

Oscar B. Ilthma

Allen Dale June

Alfred Leonard

Johnny R. Manuelito

William McCabe

Chester Nez

Jack Nez

Lloyd Oliver

Frank Denny Pete

Balmer Slowtalker, aka Joe Palmer

Nelson S. Thompson

Harry Tsosie

John W. Willie, Jr.

Bill Dene Yazzie, aka William Dean Wilson

These were men with a rich cultural Diné history. They were sons, brothers, fathers, grandfathers, teachers, and protectors. They were leaders, naat'aanii [naa-taa-NEE]. After military service, they built careers in politics, law enforcement, education, translation, art, and traditional healing. Some enjoyed work as mechanics, janitors, and butchers. Some even worked on the railroad. They lived with valor and heroism, yet their Diné upbringing and teachings helped them remain humble.

Code Talkers Peter Nakaidinae, Joseph P. Gatewood, and Lloyd Oliver, 1943

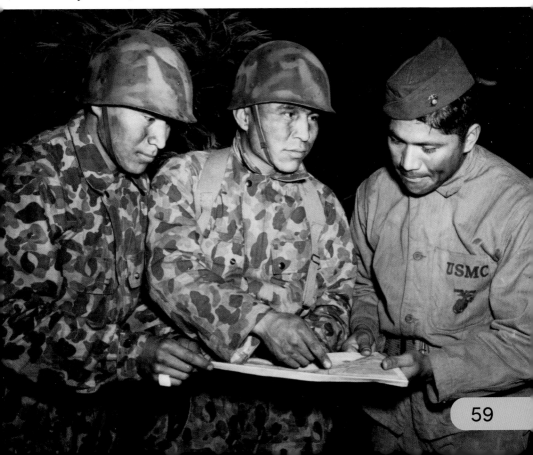

Life on the reservation was hard, and life in boarding schools was even more difficult. The endurance and struggles these men faced in youth prepared them for life in the military. Their Diné culture gave them the knowledge and skills they needed to create and utilize an unbreakable code that saved lives. The strength and endurance they built have served them well in their adult lives and into old age. May we continue to observe and celebrate their resiliency.

I opened by welcoming you to learn about the Navajo Code Talkers in a good manner. Now, we close with the Diné phrase hágoónee' [HAH-goh-uh-neh] to say, "See you later, okay," or "All right, then." I hope you learned about how Navajo culture shaped and supported the Navajo Code Talkers.

—Danielle C. Burbank

MY CLANS:
Hashk'ąąn Hadzohí nishłį. Tsé Ńjíkiní éí báshíshchíín. Tábąąhí dashicheii. Dziłtł'ahnii dashinálí.

I am Yucca Fruit clan. I am born for Cliff Dweller. My maternal grandfathers are Water's Edge. My paternal grandfathers are Mountain Cove.

The author (front) with her father, Daniel Johnson, her aunt, Bertie Johnson, and her grandfather, Deswood R. Johnson, Sr.

GLOSSARY

Assimilate
To change one's culture to match the culture of those around them

Bilingual
Able to speak two languages

Character
A symbol that represents a sound in a language

Discipline
Strict training that may involve punishment

Identity
Sense of one's self

Legacy
The lasting ideas or achievements left by a person after they die

Lifeways
In Indigenous cultures, the teachings and practices of the people

Mandatory
Required; without a choice

Matrilineal
Following the mother's side of a family

Missionary
A person who teaches others about their religion

Oral tradition
Sharing stories verbally, from memory

Paternal
Related to one's father

Persevere
To work without giving up, even when something is difficult

Platoon
A group in a military unit

Recruit
To ask someone to join

Reservation
Land defined by a treaty and assigned to a tribal nation

Revitalization
Bringing something back after it had faded away or weakened

Rigorous
Challenging and strict

Tribal nation
An Indigenous tribe within the US

Valor
Bravery

Vocational school
A school that teaches practical skills for a future career or job

INDEX

QUIZ

Answer the questions to see what you have learned. Check your answers in the key below.

1. What war were the Navajo Code Talkers a part of?

2. How many Navajo were in the first group of Code Talkers?

3. Which three states include the Navajo Nation?

4. What word did the Navajo Code Talkers use for tank?

5. In what year was the Navajo code declassified?

1. World War II 2. 29 3. Arizona, New Mexico, Utah 4. Tortoise 5. 1968

Answers, p. 8: 1. Navajo 2. Marines 3. Code